# LOCAL HISTORY REPRINTS

316 GREEN LANE, STREATHAM, LONDON SW16 3AS

Originally printed in 1792 by
A. Strahan for T. Cadell in the Strand
as part of
The Environs of London :
being an historical account of the Towns, Villages, and Hamlets
within 12 miles of that Capital;
interspersed with biographical anecdotes
by
The Rev. Daniel Lysons, A.M., F.A.S.


This editon published in 1991 by
Local History Reprints
316 Green Lane
Streatham
London SW16  3AS


ISBN 1 85699 018 4

# INTRODUCTION

Daniel Lysons was born on the 28th April 1762, the eldest son of Samuel Lysons, the Rector of Rodmarton and Cherrington in Gloucestershire. He was educated at Bath Grammar School and Oxford.

He followed his fathers profession into the church, his first appointment being as curate to Mortlake in 1784, which was followed in 1790 by the position of curate of Putney.

It was whilst resident in Putney that he started his survey of the environs of London. He was greatly encouraged in this work by Horace Walpole, Earl of Orford, who appointed him his chaplain, and to whom his work was dedicated.

This was a monumental undertaking which was to consume him until the turn of the 19th Century. During the period 1792 to 1796 he published four volumes detailing a historical account of all the towns, villages and hamlets within 12 miles of London. These include a number of illustrations many of which were drawn and sketched by Daniel himself.

The first volume covered the locations in Surrey, which was followed in 1795 by two Middlesex volumes, with the fourth book in the series covering the counties of Hertfordshire, Essex and Kent being published in 1796. In 1800 he issued an extra volume detailing further parishes in Middlesex which had been left out of his two previous volumes.

In 1811 a second edition of his work was published together with a supplement consisting of additions and corrections to the original work.

The Environs of London quickly established itself as an authoritative topographical source, and in the case of the Surrey volume, provided the first major work on the villages in the northern part of the County since Aubrey's Natural History and Antiquities of the County of Surrey which was first published in 1718.

Lysons account of Mitcham provides us with considerably more information than Aubrey's book, which principally lists monumental inscriptions in the parish church and graveyard.

Lysons gives us a brief history of the various manors in the parish, and he tells us that in 1792, the population of Mitcham numbered only 3,240 people who occupied just 540 buildings.

He mentions that about 250 acres of the parish were occupied by physic gardens, with more than 100 acres of this total being reserved for the growing of peppermint which was much used in making "a cordial well-known to the dram-drinkers".

On the remaining acreage, wormwood, camomile, aniseed, rhubarb, liquorice "and many other medicinal plants in great abundance" were grown.

Lysons tells us of the visit made to Mitcham by Queen Elizabeth I in 1598 when she came to stay at the house of Sir Julius Caesar, the Master of the Rolls. In his account of the visit, Sir Julius tells us of the expense he incurred in accommodating the Royal party overnight. This exceeded £700, a considerable sum of money for those days. Sir Julius writes:

"Tuesday Sept 12 the Queen visited my house at Micham, and supped and lodged there, and dined there the next day. I presented her with a gown of cloth of silver richly embroidered; a black net-work mantle with pure gold; a taffeta hat, white, with several flowers, and a jewel of gold set therein with rubies and diamonds. Her Majesty removed from my house after dinner the 13th of September to Nonsuch, with exceeding good contentment, which entertainment of her majesty, with the former disappointment, amounted to £700 sterling, besides mine own provisions and what was sent to me by my friends."

We also learn that Sir Walter Raleigh had a house and estate at Mitcham through his marriage to Queen Elizabeth's maid of honour, the daughter of Sir Nicholas Throgmorton. This estate was sold for £2,500 when Raleigh was preparing for his expedition to Guiana.

Daniel Lysons was a highly respected topographical and historical researcher of his day, becoming a Fellow of the Society of Antiquaries in 1790, and a Fellow of the Royal Society in 1797.

When his uncle died in 1800, Daniel inherited Hempstead Court and the family estates in Gloucestershire. Having secured a sound financial base through his inheritance he was able to consider marriage, and on 12th May 1801 he wed Sarah Hardy, the eldest daughter of Lt. Col. Thomas Carteret Hardy of the York Fusiliers. In 1804 he succeeded to the family living at Rodmarton in Gloucestershire. Sarah bore him four children, two sons and two daughters before she died in 1808.

Daniel married for a second time on 2nd July 1813, when he took as his bride Josepha Catherine Susanna Cooper, the daughter of John Gilbert Cooper of Thurgarton Priory in Nottinghamshire. Josepha bore him a son in 1816, who was christened Daniel, and who rose to the rank of general in the army and become constable of the Tower of London.

Lysons died on 3rd January 1834 at Hempstead Court and was buried in the family grave at Rodmarton in Gloucestershire.

**JOHN W BROWN**

# THE
# *ENVIRONS* of *LONDON:*
### BEING
## AN HISTORICAL ACCOUNT
#### OF THE
## TOWNS, VILLAGES, AND HAMLETS,
### Within Twelve Miles of that Capital;
#### *INTERSPERSED WITH BIOGRAPHICAL ANECDOTES.*

By the Rev. DANIEL LYSONS, A.M. F.A.S.
Chaplain to the Right Hon. the Earl of ORFORD.

### VOLUME THE FIRST.
## *COUNTY OF SURREY.*

*View of Putney from the Bishop of London's Lawn at Fulham.*

## LONDON:
PRINTED BY A. STRAHAN, FOR T. CADELL IN THE STRAND.
MDCCXCII.

FARI·QUÆ SENTIAT

ANECDOTES OF PAINTING

TO

*The Right Honourable*

HORACE

EARL OF ORFORD,

BARON WALPOLE OF HOUGHTON,

*in the County of Norfolk,*

THIS WORK

*is respectfully inscribed*

*by* his Lordſhip's

*obliged humble Servant,*

THE AUTHOR.

# ADVERTISEMENT.

WHILST a tafte for local hiftory fo generally prevails, it is fomewhat fingular that the counties adjacent to London fhould not have had their due fhare of illuftration; for even in thofe of which hiftories have been publifhed, fome very interefting particulars have been wholly unnoticed. The author of the following work offers to the public what he has been able to collect, relating either to the ancient hiftory or prefent ftate of the feveral parifhes within twelve miles of the capital, a diftrict which furnifhes perhaps more curious and interefting matter for obfervation than any other of the fame extent in the kingdom. A brief defcription of the fituation, foil, produce, and manufactures; the defcent of the principal, particularly manerial property; the parifh churches, and ecclefiaftical hiftory; the ftate of population, and the biography connected with each parifh; are the principal objects of the following work.

Through

# ADVERTISEMENT.

Through the obliging permiſſion of Thomas Aſtle, Eſq. John Caley, Eſq. and John Kipling, Eſq. to infpect the Records at the Tower, the Augmentation Office, and the Rolls; through the politeneſs of the preſent proprietors of the ſeveral manors, and the ready and liberal aſſiſtance of the gentlemen of the law ; the author has been enabled to give the deſcent of property in a manner which, though brief, he hopes will be found accurate. In the deſcription of pariſh churches, thoſe epitaphs only are given at length, which are either ſingular in themſelves, or record perſons of eminence, and theſe have been all copied on the ſpot; from the others he has inſerted the names of the perſons recorded, with the date of their deceaſe, merely to denote the place of interment of the ſeveral families. In treating of the eccleſiaſtical hiſtory, an account is given of the nature of the benefice of each pariſh, and, where it could be aſcertained, the deſcent of the advowſon. In this department, the frequent references to the MSS. in the Lambeth library will ſhew how much the author has been indebted to his Grace the Archbiſhop of Canterbury, for his permiſſion to conſult them. The ſucceſſion of incumbents on each benefice has not been given, on a preſumption, that a bare liſt of names would be very un-

interefting

## ADVERTISEMENT.

interefting to the reader, and tend to fwell the volume
to very little purpofe; the author has confined himfelf therefore to the noticing fuch perfons only as have
been in any refpect eminent. The parochial regifters
(for a ready accefs to which, as well as for other occa-
fional information, he is much indebted to his bre-
thren the clergy) have been found of much affiftance
in afcertaining the comparative ftate of population,
and furnifhing hints for biographical matter. The
ravages of the plague in many of the parifhes at various periods, have been afcertained from the fame
fource of information; and fuch inftances of longevity
as are there recorded, have been alfo noticed. From
the churchwardens accounts, particularly at Lambeth
and Kingfton, feveral curious circumftances, relating
to the price of provifions, and local cuftoms, have
been extracted.

The difficulty of correctnefs in a work of this nature, wherein the references are neceffarily fo numerous, is well known. The reader, it is hoped, will
excufe fuch trifling inaccuracies as may have efcaped
the author's obfervation; efpecially as he has endea-
voured to correct thofe which are material, particularly in the references to public records, which have
been

ADVERTISEMENT.

been again carefully collated with the originals, fince
the work was printed.

Of the plates fomething perhaps fhould be faid: the
portraits which reprefent perfons of confiderable eminence, are now for the firft time engraved; the others
will, it is prefumed, be found faithful delineations of
what they are intended to reprefent.

Mitcham Grove in 1796
The seat of Henry Hoare Esq.

# MITCHAM.

THIS place in Doomſday Book is called Michelham, that is, the great dwelling. In all the early records, and in many of a more recent date, it is written Miccham or Micham; the preſent mode of ſpelling, which is more remote from its etymology, was not univerſally adopted before this century.

Name.

Situation.

Boundaries, &c.

Mitcham lies in the hundred of Croydon, about 9 miles from Weſtminſter Bridge. The pariſh is bounded by Streatham on the eaſt; by Beddington, Carſhalton, and Croydon on the ſouth; Mordon on the weſt; and Merton on the north. The arable land exceeds the paſture in a conſiderable proportion. The greateſt part of the extenſive common between this place and Beddington is in Mitcham pariſh. The ſoil conſiſts principally of a rich black mould. About 250 acres are occupied by the phyſic gardeners, who cultivate lavender, wormwood, camomile, aniſeed, rhubarb, liquorice, and many other medicinal plants, in great abundance; but principally peppermint, of which there are above 100 acres. The demand for this herb is not confined to the apothecaries ſhops, it being much uſed in making a cordial well-known to the dram-drinkers. Forty years ſince, a few acres only were employed in the cultivation of medicinal herbs in this pariſh. Perhaps there is no place where it is now ſo extenſive. Mitcham is aſſeſſed the ſum of 635 l. 13 s. 0 d. to the land-tax, which in the year 1791 was at the rate of 1 s. 6 d. in the pound.

Phyſic gardeners.

Manors.

It appears that, at the time of the Conqueror's Survey, there were two manors in Mitcham, each of which was of the value of 40 s. One had been held by Brictric of the Confeſſor, and was then held of of the Bifhop of Baieux, by the canons of that convent. The other had been held by Lemarus of King Edward; and was then the property of William the fon of Anfculf. There were likewife two other manors at Witford[1] in this parifh, held by the fame perfons; the one of 30 s. the other of 40 s. value. The fmaller was the property of the canons of Baieux. I have not been able, through the deficiency of records, to trace the defcent of thefe manors fatisfactorily. Probably fome, if not all of them, reverted foon after the Conqueft to the crown. I find feveral grants by Henry I. of lands at Mitcham to be held *in capite*, viz. two hides to Robert the fon of Wolfward, and Walter le Poure[2]; one hide to Robert and Matthew de Micham[3], &c. &c. Alexander de Witford, about the fame time, held a knight's fee in Mitcham of the barony of Roger de Sumery, and of the honour of Dudley[4]. John de Aperdele is faid to have held the manor of Mitcham in 1367[5]. William Mareis had very confiderable property there in the reign of Edward III.[6] In a record 4 Richard II.[7] the manor is faid to have been divided between the King, the Earl of Glocefter, and the Prior of Merton. The Prior of Southwark is omitted, though that monaftery had a manor there at a much earlier period. The Earl of Glocefter's lands there were annexed to his manor of Camberwell[8]. Thomas Plomer, Efq. who died 15 Car. I. was feized of lands in Mitcham held of that manor[9]. The Prior of Merton held lands there about the year 1250 of William Mauduit, afterwards Earl of Warwick, by the fervice of rendering a pair of gilt fpurs[10]. William Figge[11], who died 24 Edw. III.

[1] There is no fuch hamlet now in the parifh, but a lane between Upper and Lower Mitcham ftill retains the name.
[2] Harleian MSS. Brit. Muf. N° 313. f. 20.
[3] Ibid. f. 22. b.
[4] Ibid. f. 15.
[5] Harleian MSS. N° 6281.
[6] Cl. 35 Edw. III. m. 3.
[7] Harleian MSS. Brit. Muf. N° 6281.

[8] Court Rolls of the manor of Camberwell Buckingham's.
[9] Cole's Efcheats, N° 410. Harleian MSS. Brit. Muf.
[10] Cotton MSS. Brit. Muf. Cleopatra, C. vii. f. 116.
[11] A fmall common in this parifh went by the name of Figg's-marfh, now ufually called Pig's-marfh.

was

was feized of a houfe and lands at Mitcham, which he held by the
fervice of receiving the King's diftraints for the hundred of Wallington ". Agnes, wife of Geoffry Prior, who died 7 Henry IV.
held a houfe and lands by the fame fervice ". In the year 1240 an
affize of common of pafture was taken, in which the priors of Merton and Southwark and other freeholders of the parifh of Mitcham
were plaintiffs, and William Hufcarl, Agnes Hufcarl, and others, of
Beddington and Wallington, defendants; in which the plaintiffs
gained their caufe and recovered 40 s. damages ".

There are now three diftinct manors in this parifh; the manor of
Mitcham or Canon; the manor of Bigging and Tamworth; and
the manor of Ravenfbury.

Manor of
Mitcham or
Canon.

The manor of Mitcham or Canon belonged to the Priory of St.
Mary Overie, and was granted at the diffolution of that monaftery to
Nicholas Spackman " and Chriftopher Harbottle, who alienated it to
Lawrence Warren "; from him it paffed to Nicholas Burton of Car-
fhalton ". Sir Henry Burton, K. B. fold it to Sir Nicholas Carew
in the year 1619 ". His fon Sir Francis Carew, K. B. gave it to
Thomas Temple, Efq. as a portion with his daughter Rebecca.
Mr. Temple alienated it to the Hammond family; in 1656 Thomas
Hammond, Efq. fold it to Robert Cranmer, Merchant of London ",
and it is now the property of his defcendant James Cranmer, Efq.
The fallacy of the tradition, that this was the private eftate of Arch-
bifhop Cranmer, will appear from the foregoing account of its defcent. In 1291 this manor was valued at 20 s. per annum ".

Manor of
Bigging and
Tamworth.

The manor of Bigging and Tamworth belonged to Merton Abbey,
and was granted by Henry VIII. after the fuppreffion of that mo-

¹¹ Efch. 23 Edw. III. pt. 2. N° 15.
¹² Efch. 6 Henry IV. N° 45.
¹³ Cotton MSS. Brit. Muf. Cleopatra,
C. vii. fol. 127. a.
¹⁴ Pat. 36 Hen. VIII. pt. 23. Sep. 28.
¹⁵ Pat. 5 Edw. VI. pt. 2. July 1.
¹⁶ Terrier of Lands in Surrey, Brit. Muf.

N° 4705. Ayfcough's Cat.
¹⁷ The account of this and the fubfequent
alienations was obligingly communicated by
the prefent proprietor.
¹⁸ From the information of James Cranmer,
Efq.
¹⁹ See note, p. 10.

naftery

naſtery to Robert Wilford, merchant taylor, for the ſum of 486 l. 14 s.[20] In 1569 it appears to have been the property of John Lord Mordaunt, in right of his wife[21]. In 1582 Henry Whitney, Eſq. held a court as lord of this manor, though it appears that he purchaſed a moiety thereof the enſuing year of Robert Aprece, Eſq. The Whitneys alienated the manor in 1603 to Sir John Carrill. Three years afterwards it belonged to John Lord Hunſdon, whoſe ſon ſold it in 1614 to Sir Nicholas Carew, alias Throckmorton. It was alienated about the year 1655 to Edward Thurland, Eſq. and continued in the ſame family till 1744, when it was purchaſed of the deviſees of another Edward Thurland by John Manſhip, Eſq. father of the preſent proprietor. In 1291 it was valued at 25 s. per annum.

The earlieſt proprietor of the manor of Ravenſbury that I find on record is William de Mara, or De la Mar, who was lord thereof 1250[22]. John De la Mar, and Petronilla his wife, had a grant of free warren in the pariſh of Mitcham in the reign of Edward I.[23] The manor of Ravenſbury was the property of John De la Pole Earl of Lincoln, temp. Hen. VII. and was granted after his attainder to Simon Digby[24]. It afterwards belonged to Charles Brandon Duke of Suffolk, who ſold it to Sir Nicholas Carew, 22 Henry VIII. for 800 l.[25] Upon the attainder of Sir Nicholas it was ſeized by the crown, and was granted upon leaſe[26], but was afterwards reſtored to Sir Francis Carew by Queen Mary[27], and has deſcended in the ſame manner as the Beddington eſtates.

Manor of Ravenſbury.

[20] Pat. 36 Hen. VIII. pt. 27. May 19.
[21] Extracts from the Court Rolls of the Manor, communicated by Mr. R. Barnes, the ſteward. The whole of the following account is derived from the ſame ſource.
[22] Cotton MSS. Brit. Muſ. Cleopatra, C. vii. f. 111, 112.

[23] Cart. 11 Edw. I. N° 24.
[24] Pat. 3 Hen. VII. pt. 2. Mar. 25.
[25] Cotton Cart. Antiq. Brit. Muſ. xii. 24.
[26] Pat. 34 Hen. VIII. pt. 3. Dec. 7.
[27] Orig. 1. Mar. p. 3. Rot. 38. Lord Treaſurer's Remembrancer's Office.

Sir

Sir Walter Raleigh had a houfe and eftate at Mitcham in right of his wife, who was a daughter of Sir Nicholas Throgmorton, and had been maid of honour to Queen Elizabeth. The eftate was fold with her confent for 2500 l. when he was preparing for his expedition to Guiana [28]. A houfe, in the occupation of Mr. Dempfter, who keeps an academy there, is ftill called Raleigh Houfe.

Sir Julius Cæfar, Mafter of the Rolls, had alfo a houfe here, of which he became poffeffed by an intermarriage with Mrs. Dent, the widow of a merchant whofe property it was. In 1598 he was honoured with a vifit from Queen Elizabeth, of which the following account is given in his own words [29].

" Tuefday Sept. 12. the Queen vifited my houfe at Micham, " and fupped and lodged there, and dined there the next day. I " prefented her with a gown of cloth of filver richly embroidered ; a " black net-work mantle with pure gold ; a taffeta hat, white, with " feveral flowers, and a jewel of gold fet therein with rubies and " diamonds. Her Majefty removed from my houfe after dinner " the 13th of September to Nonfuch, with exceeding good content- " ment, which entertainment of her Majefty, with the former dif- " appointment [30], amounted to 700 l. fterling, befides mine own " provifions and what was fent unto me by my friends."

The celebrated Dr. Donne refided for fome time at Mitcham [31]. Sir George More of Lofely, whofe daughter he had privately married, was fo much exafperated, that he not only refufed to forgive, but employed his utmoft endeavours to ruin him ; and actually procured his removal from the family of Lord Chancellor Ellefmere, to whom he was fecretary. At this juncture Sir Francis Wolley took compaffion on him, and received him and his family into his

Sir Walter
Raleigh.

Sir Julius
Cæfar.

Vifit of
Queen Eliza-
beth.

Dr. Donne.

---

[28] Biograph. Brit.

[29] MS. of Sir Julius Cæfar's, Brit. Muf. N° 4160. Ayfcough's Cat.

[30] In a letter from Rowland White to Sir Robert Sidney, dated Sept. 30, 1596, the Queen's intention to vifit Mitcham is mentioned, at which time probably the difappointment here alluded to happened. Sidney State Papers, vol. ii. p. 5.

[31] Biograph. Brit. and England's Worthies.

houfe,

houfe, where they continued as long as Sir Francis lived. At his death, being left deftitute of an afylum, Donne took a fmall houfe at Mitcham, " a place, as his biographers obferve, noted for good " air and choice company." Being very learned in the civil law, he was occafionally confulted by perfons of the firft rank, who paid him liberally for his advice; but this yielded only a precarious fupport, and he was fometimes reduced to great diftrefs, as may be feen by the following extract from a letter to a friend dated from this place.

" The reafon why I did not fend an anfwer to your laft week's
" letter was, becaufe it found me under too great a fadnefs; and
" at prefent it is thus with me. There is not one perfon well
" but myfelf of my family: I have already loft half a child, and
" with that mifchance of her's, my wife has fallen into fuch a dif-
" compofure as would afflict her too extremely, but that the ficknefs
" of all her other children ftupifies her, one of which in good faith
" I have not much hopes of, and thefe meet with a fortune fo ill
" provided for phyfic and fuch relief, that if God fhould eafe us
" with burials, I know not how to perform even that; but I flatter
" myfelf with this hope—that I am dying too—for I cannot wafte
" fafter than by fuch griefs.——From my hofpital at Mitcham,
                              " John Donne [32]."

Mr. Donne continued at Mitcham about two years, during which time he became fo attached to his fituation that he would have ftaid there for life had it not been for the importunity of his friends, and the generofity of Sir Robert Drury, who lent him a houfe in Drury Lane. Sir George More at laft relented, and gave him an annuity; and Donne, who had diftinguifhed himfelf by fome theological writings, at the earneft defire of King James entered into holy orders, and was afterwards made Dean of St. Paul's.

[32] This Letter is printed in the Biograph. Brit. and in Donne's Letters to eminent Perfons.

Mofes Men-
dez.

Mofes Mendez, the rich poet, who died in 1758, was an inhabit-
ant of this place. He was created M. A. at Oxford in 1750, and
was author of fome dramatic pieces, a poem called Henry and
Blanche, and various other performances, fome of which are to be
found in Dodfley's Collection.

The church.

The church, which is dedicated to St. Peter and St. Paul, is built
principally of flints, and confifts of a nave, two aifles, and a chancel;
at the eaft end of the fouth aifle is a fquare embattled tower with
a turret. The nave is feparated from the aifles by octagonal pillars,
and pointed arches. The wall of the north aifle has been rebuilt.
The church received confiderable damage by lightning in the year
1637, at which time thirteen churches in this county are faid to
have experienced the fame fate [33]. A fimilar accident happened at
Mitcham a few years fince, when the lightning entered through the
fouth wall of the tower, but without doing much injury.

Monuments.

In the chancel are the monuments of Thomas Pynner, Efq. chief
clerk comptroller to Queen Elizabeth, who died in 1583; Theophi-
lus Brereton, Efq. who died in 1638; Sir Ambrofe Crowley, alder-
man of London, (celebrated in the Tatler [34] under the name of Sir
Humphry Greenhat,) who died in 1713; and Jofeph Cranmer, Efq.
who died in 1722. There are alfo two achievements, with infcrip-
tions to the memory of John Eldred, Efq. who died in 1649, and
Mary wife of Robert Cranmer, Efq. who died in 1665. Within
the rails of the altar is the tomb of Lieut. Gen. Daniel Harvey,
governor of Guernfey, who died in 1732; in the chancel alfo are
thofe of Elizabeth wife of William Myers, Efq. who died in 1765;
and George Smith, Gent. who died in 1714.

Againft the wall at the eaft corner of the nave is the monument
of William Myers, Efq. who died in 1742; againft a north pillar
that of Bridget wife of Gabriel Glover, Efq. who died in 1709.

[33] Aubrey's Antiquities of Surrey, vol. ii. p. 143.    [34] Nᵒ 73.

In the nave was formerly a brafs plate to the memory of John Roche, an officer in the houfehold of Catherine Queen of England, who died in 1430; the infcription is preferved in Aubrey's Antiquities of Surrey.

In the eaft window of the north aifle are fome remains of painted glafs, reprefenting angels playing on mufical inftruments. Under the window is an altar tomb, from which all the brafs plates have been torn except the infcription, which is to the memory of Richard Illyngworth, who died in 1487; near this tomb is a brafs plate upon a flat ftone, to the memory of Ralph Illyngworth, Efq. who died in 1572. Againft the north wall are the monuments of Henry Allcraft, Efq. who died in 1779; the Reverend John Evanfon, vicar of Mitcham for the fpace of 44 years, who died in 1778; and Benjamin Tate, Efq. who died in 1790. In the fame aifle are flat ftones in memory of Jofeph Taylor, merchant, who died in 1732; John Robinfon, merchant, who died in 1750; and Denzil Onflow, Efq. who died in 1765.

At the weft end of the north aifle ftands the font, which is ornamented with Gothic tracery, and refembles that at Mortlake which was erected in the reign of Henry VI.

At the eaft end of the fouth aifle is a tablet to the memory of John Cloberry Gafcoigne, who died in 1776.

In the church-yard is the tomb of Anne Hallam, an actrefs, with the following infcription:

> " Chariffimæ fuæ uxori
> " Annæ Hallam, Hiftrioni,
> " Ultimum hoc amoris munus
> " Mæftiffimus dedit
> " Gulielmus Hallam.

" Intravit } Anno { 1696 } Æt. 44."
" Exit    }       { 1740 }

Tomb of Anne Hallam.

Mrs.

Mrs. Hallam belonged to Covent-Garden Theatre, where fhe acquired confiderable celebrity by her performance of Lady Macbeth. She was much admired alfo in the character of Lady Touchwood.

In the church-yard are the tombs likewife of John Bligh, M. D. who died in 1678; Frances Auftin of Peterborough, who died in 1734; Charles Dubois, Efq. who died in 1740; Waldo Dubois, Efq. and Ebenezer Dubois, Efq. who died in 1746; Peter Waldo, Efq. who died in 1762; William Tate, Efq. who died in 1781; and John Twyne, Efq. who died in 1783.

Rectory and vicarage.

The church of Mitcham is in the diocefe of Winchefter and the deanery of Ewell. The benefice is a vicarage. The rectory belonged to the monaftery of St. Mary Overie, and has undergone the fame alienations as the manor of Canon, being now impropriated to James Cranmer, Efq. who is patron of the vicarage. The rectory was taxed in 1291 at 20 marks[33]. The profits of the vicarage have been lately much improved by the increafe of the phyfic gardens, the tithes of which form a principal part of its revenues. It was taxed in 1291 at 8 marks. In the king's books it is reckoned amongft the difcharged livings, and is faid to be 35 l. clear yearly value.

Anthony Sadler.

Anthony Sadler, who was inftituted to the vicarage in 1661, publifhed feveral fermons; a pamphlet againft the commiffioners who fat at Whitehall for the approbation of minifters; " A Divine " Mafque," dedicated to General Monk; and a pamphlet entitled " Strange News indeed from Micham in Surrey of the treacherous " and barbarous Proceedings of Robert Cranmer, Merchant of Lon- " don, againft A. Sadler, Vicar of Micham, London, 1664." In this pamphlet Mr. Cranmer is accufed of many cruel and unjuft perfecutions of the vicar, particularly of throwing him into prifon, and inducing him, under falfe pretences, to fubfcribe a bond for 500 l. which threatened himfelf and family with ruin. An anfwer

[33] See note, p. 10.

appeared

appeared foon afterwards entitled, " The Sadler fadled," being a
vindication of Mr. Cranmer's conduct, who it feems prefented Sadler to the vicarage, then worth only 40 l. per annum. The vicar
was not long fettled there before he inftituted a fuit againft his patron for dilapidations and facrilege, and by his behaviour rendered
himfelf odious to all his parifhioners; at length terms of reconci-
liation were agreed upon; one of which was, that Mr. Sadler
fhould refign the vicarage at a certain time, and he entered into a
bond of 500 l. for that purpofe. It appears that upon his refufing
to quit the vicarage, he was threatened with the penalty of the bond.
He kept poffeffion however till his death, which happened four
years afterwards, in the year 1669. Anthony Wood fays, that he
left behind him, " the character of a man of a rambling head, and
" a turbulent fpirit [36]."

The prefent vicar is the Reverend Streynfham Derbyfhire Myers.
The parifh regifter commences in the year 1650.

Parifh regif-
ter.

|  | Average of Baptifms. | Average of Burials. |
|---|---|---|
| 1680—1689 | 29 |  |
| 1705—1714 |  | 37 |
| 1780—1789 | 97 | 94 |

Comparative
ftate of popu-
lation.

The entries of burials, during the latter part of the laft century,
and till the year 1705, are imperfect.

The prefent number of houfes in Mitcham is about 540.

The number of burials in 1665 were 21; in 1666, 24; not exceeding the average of that period. It appears neverthelefs that the
village was not free from the plague, a man and his four fons, " who
" died of the ficknefs," having been buried in one night.

The two following are the only entries in the regifter which are
any way fingular:

" Anne the daughter of George Wafhford, who had 24 fingers
" and toes, baptized Oct. 19, 1690."

[36] Athen. Oxon. vol. ii. col. 675.

" Widow

" Widow Durant, aged 103 years, buried Sep. 23, 1711."

Mr. Henry Smith, who is erroneoufly faid by Aubrey to have omitted this parifh in his numerous benefactions to the county of Surrey, left 4 l. per annum to poor houfekeepers. Thomas Plummer[37], Efq. left 5l. per annum to buy bread for the poor; Mrs. Rofamond Oxtoby, who died in 1792, left 2 l. 12 s. per ann. for the fame purpofe. Mrs. Fifher, in the year 1709, left 200 l. to purchafe lands, the annual rent of which fhould be diftributed amongft poor houfekeepers : this charity produces about 14 l. per annum.

Sunday-
fchool.
The inhabitants of Mitcham fupport a Sunday-fchool by voluntary contributions, upon an extenfive plan. A fchool-houfe was built for that purpofe in the year 1788.

Mitcham
Grove.
Mitcham Grove, a pleafant villa on the north fide of the road to Sutton, was a few years fince the property and refidence of Lord Loughborough, by whom it was fold to Henry Hoare, Efq. the prefent proprietor.

Manufacto-
ries.
In this parifh are fome fnuff-mills, and Mr. Rucker's and Mr. Fenning's manufactories for printing calicoes.

Workhoufe.
A large workhoufe was built in the year 1782 on the fide of Mitcham Common, at the expence of 1,200 l. The average number of the poor who are placed there is about feventy.

[37] He is called Plomer in the record quoted p. 351. by which it appears that he died in 1639.

# APPENDIX.

## MITCHAM.

**Manor of Ravenſbury.**

Sir John Burgherſhe died 15 Ric. II. ſeized of the manor of Ra-venſbury [75], which deſcended to John Arundell, who married Mar-garet his daughter and heir [76]. It was held under Baldwin Frevylle, as of his manor of Aſhted [77].

**Ancient houſe.**

There is an ancient houſe at Mitcham, the property of Mrs. Sarah Chandler, widow of George Chandler, Eſq. in which are the remains of a chapel. The proprietors of this houſe, which is held under the Dean and Chapter of Canterbury, claim a right to the north aiſle of the church, in ſupport of which it appears that the family of Illyngworth, who were buried in that aiſle in the ſixteenth century, held a houſe and lands under the church of Canterbury, temp. Edw. IV. [78] It is probable that it was at an earlier period the pro-perty of Henry Strete, who had a licence for an oratory in his houſe at Mitcham, in the year 1348 [79].

[75] Eſch. 15 Ric. II. N° 8.
[76] Eſch. 2 Hen. VI. N° 39.
[77] Now in the tenure of Mr. Worsfold.

[78] Eſch. 16 Edw. IV. N° 38.
[79] Regiſt. Winton. W. de Edindon, pt. 2. f. 20. b.

Mitcham as shown on a map of Surrey dated 1792